16/₇.
3d

Sandi Toksvig's
GUIDE TO
SPAIN

This activity book belongs to:

....

RED FOX

DRAW A CIRCLE ON THE MAP WHERE YOU ARE GOING IN SPAIN.

FRANCE

La Coruna Gijon San Sebastian
Bilbao
Vigo Leon Pamplona

PORTUGAL

Valladolid Zaragoza Barcelona

Salamanca Segovia

Madrid

Toledo Valencia

Olivenza Albacete

Alicante

Cordoba
Huelva Seville Granada Mojocar
Malaga Almeria

ALGERIA

Population: About 40.5 million

Language: Spanish (obviously).

Size: 314,387 miles² (505,957 km²)

Coastline: 3,084 miles (4,964 km)

Capital City: Madrid

Population of Madrid: About 3 million

Currency: Euro (€). There are 100 cents in 1 Euro.

2

Welcome to Spain or España!

There is so much to see and do in Spain! This guide will help you to remember where you went and what you did – make sure you write in your journal on pages 13–14. You can even learn how to say things in Spanish and there are a few games and activities just to make sure you never get bored. I'll also tell you some quite interesting things about the country and the people who live here. Did you know that:

Spain has the second highest number of heritage sites in the world so there is a lot of history. People have lived in Spain for about as long as there have been people. A lot of them came during the last ice age – probably because of the weather.

Spain is a high place. It has an average altitude of 660 metres. Only Switzerland is higher. There are forests, rivers and valleys. You can go fishing, biking, hiking, riding, skiing or look at some of the animals, like bison.

[What's the difference between a buffalo and a bison? You can't wash your hands in a buffalo.]

There is a festival (fiesta) somewhere practically every week, where anything can happen – from streets being carpeted in flowers to cows being given as presents. In Buñol there's even a huge tomato fight!

I'm sure you'll see masses of exciting things during your stay and have lots of fun. Make sure you write them all down in this book. Now, follow me and let's find out more about Spain!

Sandi Toksvig

There are lots of different ways to get to Spain, and the cities and villages there. How did you travel?

By Plane

There are around 47 airports in Spain. The biggest is Barajas International Airport in Madrid. The Spanish national airline is Iberia.

Can you unscramble the names of these Spanish cities where there are airports? To help you I've left the first letter as a capital letter but you can also look at the map on page 2.

By Boat

Spain has eight major ports. The largest is Bilbao, which is also the sixth biggest city.

≹ CURIOUS FACT ≺

Some of the most famous sailors in the world were Spanish. A man called Gabriel de Castilla (1577–1620) was probably the first person to see Antarctica when he got there in 1603.

1. galMaa _____

2. ecrnaoBla _____

3. Slilvee _____

4. oabliB _____

5. didMar _____

6. zilba _____

By Train

There are lots of trains in Spain, including high-speed trains called AVEs. They can do up to 186 miles (300 km) per hour, which is very fast!

By Road

To drive from the UK you would need to go through the Channel Tunnel or take a ferry and then drive through France and across the Pyrenees mountains. This would take about three days and would involve a lot of car games. In Spanish 'the car' is *el coche*.

⚡ CURIOUS FACT ⚡

Henry Ford, one of the first car makers, stuffed his seats with Spanish moss to save money. Unfortunately the soft moss also had bugs in it that led to some itchy bottoms. If anyone has an itch, ask if they have Spanish moss in their seat. Spanish moss doesn't even grow in Spain!

TRAVEL GAMES
Travelling can be a bit boring sometimes!
Here are some games that might be fun.

COUNTING DONKEYS

This game does not work well in the city. It is played by two people on opposite sides of a car. Each person counts how many donkeys they see on their side, and each donkey is one point. If, however, side A passes a cemetery on their side, then side B shouts, 'Your donkeys are buried!' and side A loses all their points. A white cow counts as a bonus of 10 points. The person with the most points at the end of the car journey wins.

TRAVEL BINGO

Make some bingo cards before you go with things you might see on the way. The first person to tick off everything on their card wins.

Here are some ideas to get you started
(see you if you can say them in Spanish too):

Restaurant	Supermarket	Church	School
restaurante	*supermercado*	*iglesia*	*escuela*
A tall person	Bicycle	Cow	Beach umbrella
persona alta	*bicicleta*	*vaca*	*sombrilla*

YOUR TICKET

Stick your train, plane or boat ticket here:

ALPHABET RACE

The aim of this game is to spot things out of the window that start with all the letters from A–Z, in order. So if you spot an alligator (not very likely), then you can tick the 'A' box and try to find something starting with B, then C, and so on. The first person to see something starting with Z wins! (If you see a zebra then you get bonus points.) If your word is in Spanish then you can skip one letter.

You can only name each object once, so you can't call the same thing three different names just to use your letters!

A

B

C

D

E

F

G

H

I

J

K

L

M

N

O

P

Q

R

S

T

U

V

W

X

Y

Z

SPANISH FACTS

The Spanish Flag

The Spanish flag is three bands of red, yellow and red with the national coat of arms in the middle. Can you see any Spanish flags where you are staying?

The National Anthem

The Spanish national anthem is *La Marcha Real* or 'the Royal March'. It is one of the few national anthems in the world to have no official lyrics! Maybe if you ask nicely, a Spanish person you meet might sing it to you and you can listen to which words they use.

Weather

People usually go to Spain for the sun but you should know they also have a lot of storms – about 10,000 a year, 5,000 of them in the summer.

⸙ CURIOUS FACT ⸙

On 17 August 2003, 60,201 bolts of lightning were counted in one day in Spain.

Money

The Spanish once used Pesetas but they now have the Euro. There are 100 cents in 1 Euro.

The sign for the Euro looks like this:

Try to get a cent coin and stick it here. (Don't do this if you are thirsty and it's the last one you've got.)

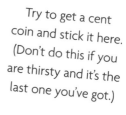

Entertainment

Spanish people like reading and going to the movies, just like you. Traditional things like Flamenco dancing and music are also popular. There are five main Spanish television channels. See if you can find out the names of some of them and write them here:

Where I Stayed

Depending what kind of holiday you are taking, you could be staying in all sorts of different places. It might be a tent, caravan, hotel or house.

I am staying...

I like it because...

Things that are close to where I am staying include...

Draw a picture here of what you can see from your bedroom window (or outside your tent!):

DIFFERENT THINGS IN SPAIN

There are some things that might be different when you're on holiday in Spain.

In Spain they drive on the right-hand side of the road, so be very careful near traffic and make sure you look in all directions when you cross.

Not everyone speaks English. Try to speak some Spanish. Even if you can just say one word! Maybe you could learn how to ask someone if they speak English: *Hablas inglés*? You might have to practise this a few times but don't give up. Ask the adult who you are with for some help.

Remember to say *Hola* when you meet someone, even a shopkeeper, for the first time. Look at pages 17–21 for some other words. Smile! Being friendly is easy, even if you can't speak the language.

There are 5,000 million trees in Spain. I can say this with confidence because I don't think you'll count. In some places there are 280 trees per person. The European average is 0.36 trees per person.

HOLA!

In many places the shops are closed in the afternoons so that everyone can relax after their lunch – they might even have a quick sleep!

Shake hands or kiss on both cheeks to say hello to a Spanish person (obviously not if it's just a waiter come to take your order).

SPOT THE DIFFERENCE

Look carefully at these two pictures of me at a Spanish market. Can you spot the differences? Circle them in picture B. There are 10 things to find.

SPANISH HOLIDAYS

Fiesta means 'holiday'. They began as religious festivals but are now more like street parties. Some are small local events and some are huge. Lots have marching bands, fireworks and dancing. Some of the biggest are:

Fallas of Valencia

On 19 March each year 350 beautifully made paper statues are burned to the ground. It's a hot party.

La Tomatina

Held in the village of Buñol near Valencia. This is the world's biggest tomato fight. Tens of thousands of people fight with truckloads of tomatoes.

Feria de Abril

This is the April Seville Fair in Seville (obviously). It lasts all week with amazing horse riding and flamenco dancing. A million people go.

Fiesta de San Fermin

Held in Pamplona and lasts one week from 7 July. Every morning at 8.00 a.m. a crowd gathers to run ahead of six fighting bulls and two herds of bullocks down to the bullfighting ring. Not everybody likes this fiesta, and it is very dangerous. Bulls are best looked at in a field and a distance.

JOURNAL

Holidays are usually so busy with lots going on that when
you get home you've forgotten what you did! Use these pages
to write a journal about the places you visited and the things you did.

JOURNAL

MADRID

Madrid is the capital of Spain and is right in the centre of the country. About three million people live there – including the Spanish royal family. It's a pretty busy place! People like to go shopping in Madrid but there are lots of things to see.

Geography: Madrid is one of the greenest cities in the world, and almost one third of the city is covered in trees. There are about 40 parks in the city, which cover about 33 million square metres. That's a lot of room to throw a ball!

Stuff you have to see (or at least tell people you've seen and buy a postcard...):

The Royal Palace: In 1734 an ancient fortress called El Alcazar burned down. Because of this, the king decided to build the Royal Palace. It has 2,800 rooms and you can take a tour to see them, which I guess takes a long time. Be glad you're not a cleaner.

Bridge of Segovia: This is the oldest bridge in Madrid.

The Prado Museum: This is *the* place for all sorts of art. They have one of the world's biggest and best collections (about 30,000 pieces so they only ever show about 10%).

Retiro Park: This is the largest park in Madrid. Here you can ride around in horse-drawn carriages or on bikes. There are also puppet shows, pavement artists and street performers to watch.

BARCELONA

Barcelona is Spain's second biggest city, and a very popular place to visit. There are two official languages spoken in Barcelona. See if you can find out what they are.

Facts about Barcelona (if you don't go there, you can use these and pretend you did!):

La Sagrada Familia is the famous church in Barcelona. They started building it in 1882 and it won't be finished until around 2020! It's not because the builders are drinking tea all day – the design is very complicated.

The Barcelona aquarium has an 80m-long shark tunnel!

Barcelona is famous for artists like Gaudí and Picasso. If you go to Barcelona, try to spot some of their artwork.

Park Güell is a popular park and a nice way to see the city because it is up on a hill. It contains huge lizards and a massive colourful bench.

La Rambla is a very busy street in Barcelona. It is filled with market stalls and shops and gets very crowded.

Barcelona has a subway system, which is the fastest way to get around.

SPEAKING IN SPANISH

The fun thing about going to Spain is that you can learn to say some words in Spanish, and have fun working out what different things mean (like signs and menus).

Speaking Spanish means you don't have to worry about writing it down. For example, writing 'Hi, how are things?' means you have to use lots of punctuation that looks strange to us: ¡Hola! ¿Qué tal? Better to just pretend you know what you are doing and speak out loud.

Here are some words that are really useful to know. Take this guide out with you so you can practise. Ask an adult to help you learn how to say the words.

English	Spanish	English	Spanish
Yes	*Sí*	**One**	*Uno*
No	*No*	**Two**	*Dos*
Please	*Por favor*	**Three**	*Tres*
Thank you	*Gracias*	**Four**	*Cuatro*
Monday	*lunes*	**Five**	*Cinco*
Tuesday	*martes*	**Six**	*Seis*
Wednesday	*miércoles*	**Seven**	*Siete*
Thursday	*jueves*	**Eight**	*Ocho*
Friday	*viernes*	**Nine**	*Nueve*
Saturday	*sábado*	**Ten**	*Diez*
Sunday	*domingo*	**Fifty**	*Cincuenta*
Chocolate	*Chocolate*	**One hundred**	*Cien*

COUNTING IN SPANISH

Look at the picture below and the items underneath. How many of each of the items can you see in the picture? Write the number in Spanish (clue: look at the list of numbers on page 17).

WHAT TO SAY

These are some simple phrases that you might want to get the hang of on holiday. Ask an adult to help you learn how to say the words.

The main thing to remember when speaking Spanish is to look very relaxed. It is often hot in Spain and you don't want to overheat yourself by talking too energetically. Try to be casual, as if you say these things every day. Spanish 'S's tend to have a bit more of a hiss than English ones, so mind you don't spray all over everyone.

My name is _____	Me llamo _____
I come from Britain	Vengo de Gran Bretaña
Where is _____ ?	¿Dónde está _____ ?
I am on holiday	Estoy de vacaciones
I would like _____	Quisiera _____
How much does _____ cost?	¿Cuánto cuesta?
Open	Abierto
Closed	Cerrado
Sweets	Dulces

Words you shouldn't ask all at the same time:

Where?	¿Donde?	When?	¿Cuando?
Why?	¿Porqué?	What?	¿Qué?
Who?	¿Quien?	How?	¿Como?

Some phrases I hope you won't need:

I'm lost	Me he perdido
Help!	Socorro!

Once you've learned how to say some simple words, here are some more important phrases to annoy adults with:

¿Hemos llegado ya?
Are we nearly there?

Todo el mundo te está mirando.
Everyone is looking at you.

La familia entera se ha perdido.
The whole family is hopelessly lost.

Realmente no conozco a nadie al que le guste mi hermana.
Actually I don't know anyone who likes my sister.

No hay papel higiénico.
There's no toilet paper.

Déjame dar une vuelta más, por favor.
Just one more ride, please.

Sí, mi hermano es un poco pesado.
Yes, my brother is annoying.

⸞ CURIOUS FACT ⸞

The country where the most people speak Spanish is not Spain. It's Mexico!

DICTIONARY

airport	aeropuerto		**mother**	madre
apple	manzana		**orange**	naranja
banana	plátano		**plane**	avión
beach	playa		**sandwich**	bocadillo
bicycle	bicicleta		**sister**	hermana
boat	barco		**sunglasses**	gafas de sol
breakfast	desayuno		**sunscreen**	bronceador
brother	hermano		**swimming**	natación
car	coche		**taxi**	taxi
caravan	caravana		**tent**	tienda de campaña
cheese	queso		**thirsty**	que tiene sed
cold	frío		**tomato**	tomate
dinner	cena		**towel**	toalla
father	padre		**train station**	estación
French fries	patatas fritas		**train**	tren
hamburger	hamburguesa		**water**	agua
hot	caliente			
hotel	hotel			
hungry	hambriento			
juice	zumo			
lunch	almuerzo			

⋛ SPANISH WORDS ⋚

Write down any other words that you see.
Add the English if you know it, or ask an adult
to help you work out what each word means:

WORD SEARCH

See if you can find these Spanish words in the puzzle below. You could even try to work out what they mean (clue: they are all contained in this activity book)

Words to find:
- ☐ gracias
- ☐ churro
- ☐ barco
- ☐ ocho
- ☐ calamares
- ☐ abierto
- ☐ fiesta
- ☐ iglesia

S	A	I	C	A	R	G	U
E	F	B	C	I	T	A	A
R	A	I	A	A	I	I	C
A	B	I	E	R	T	O	A
M	E	Z	R	S	C	C	T
A	S	U	A	H	T	O	C
L	A	T	O	C	E	A	A
A	I	S	E	L	G	I	L
C	H	U	R	R	O	A	S

SPORTS DIARY

Sport is popular in Spain, and the 1992 summer Olympics were held in Barcelona.

Football

Football is the most played sport in Spain. The Spanish football team has been in every World Cup since 1978.

FACT:
The matador's cape (which is supposed to make the bull mad) is red – but this is odd because bulls are colour-blind.

Tour of Spain

This is a big bicycle race in very tight clothes that takes three weeks. (It's just like the Tour de France except with less French bits.) It is held in September and usually finishes in Madrid.

Bullfighting (La corrida de toros)

Lots of people don't like bullfighting but it is an important part of Spanish history and culture. Why not read a bit about it and then make up your own mind? There are 43 bullfighting schools in Spain and in some you can start aged nine, though you need to be sixteen to perform. The men and women who fight the bull are called matadors.

Make a note here of all the sports you did on holiday, like swimming, skiing, walking and cycling:

ACTIVITY DIARY

Make a list here of the books and comics that you took to read on holiday:

One of the most famous Spanish books is called *Don Quijote* de la Mancha, written by Miguel de Cervantes Saavedra. It's a funny book about a man who pretends he is a knight and travels around Spain with his squire, Sancho Panza, having adventures. Cervantes was born in the Spanish city of Alcalá de Henares, where you can see wonderful statues of Don Quijote and Sancho Panza.

Writing postcards

Postcards are a nice way of telling people at home a little bit about your holiday. You can send them to your friends, grandparents or other family members. You could even send one to yourself for when you get home!

Barcelona

Postcard games

Anyone can buy a postcard with a nice view. Why not have a family competition to see who can find the worst postcard for the holiday? Find one with a picture of a petrol station or a really terrible view. The winner gets a prize like a bar of chocolate.

FOOD

Lots of people never really try Spanish food because they carry on eating chips and fast food on their holidays. This is a shame because the real Spanish food is fantastic.

Mealtimes

They may be a bit later than you are used to.

Breakfast – usually served at about 9 a.m.

Lunch – 2 p.m.

Dinner – about 9 p.m. (try not to fall asleep in your food!)

Fish and Seafood (Pescado y Mariscos)

Spanish people eat everything and anything you can imagine from the sea. Some strange things you may see include:

Vieira: a fan-shaped sea scallop

Pulpo a la gallega: Galician octopus

Boquerones: tiny fried anchovies

Calamares: rings of squid

Paella

Paella is the most famous Spanish food. It was the poor people from Valencia who discovered it by mixing rice with vegetables and leftover bits of rabbit. Now you can get it with all kinds of things, like seafood and chicken. Try some – it's very tasty!

Tapas

Tapa means 'cover' in Spanish. It used to be a snack, like a piece of ham or cheese, served free with a drink. The tapas were put on a small plate that went over the drink to keep away flies.

Olive oil (Aceite de oliva)

Central Spain is the best place in the world for growing olive trees. Olive oil is so popular that Spanish people even put it on toast in the morning for breakfast.

Saffron

This is a golden-yellow spice from crocus flowers. The flowers open at night and must be collected before dawn, otherwise they lose their flavour. Saffron is the most expensive spice in the world.

Gazpacho (Chilled tomato soup)

Gazpacho is made with soaked bread. Originally it was just bread, olive oil and crushed garlic, but now tomatoes are often added too.

FOOD

Serrano ham

This is ham made from pigs that eat lots of acorns. Acorns have a very hard shell, so don't try eating them yourself!

Fruit (Fruta)

Spain produces over 125 million kilograms of mandarins, 80–100 million kilograms of oranges and 30–40 million kilos of lemons every year.

Orange juice is *jugo de naranja*.

Desserts

Churro: a fried-dough pastry. Very good dipped in hot chocolate – yum!

Coca de albaricoque: apricot cake

Ensaimada: spiral-shaped pastry

Orejuela: honey fritter

Turrón: a bar made of ground almonds and honey. Eaten at Christmas.

Yema: egg-yolk sweet. Hmm, not sure about the sound of these…

⋛ CURIOUS FACT ⋚

The first chocolate in Europe was made in Spain. If you visit the Monasterio de Piedra (Monastery of the Rock) in the village of Nuevalos, Aragon, you can see the history of chocolate plus some great waterfalls.

WHAT'S ON THE MENU?

See if you can spot any of these things on a menu:

Arroz con leche .... **Rice pudding**

Batido de chocolate .... **Chocolate milkshake**

Chorizo .... **Spicy sausage**

Cocido .... **Chickpea and meat stew**

Ensalada .... **Salad**

Gambas .... **Prawns**

Gazpacho .... **Cold soup**

Helado .... **Ice cream**

Jamón serrano .... **Cured ham**

Queso manchego .... **Sheep's cheese**

Menú del día .... **Dish of the day**

Paella .... **Fried rice dish**

Patatas bravas .... **Spicy potatoes**

Pollo .... **Chicken**

Pulpo .... **Octopus**

Tortilla .... **Omelette**

Pies de cerdo
– you may not
want these. They
are pig's trotters.

MY FOOD DIARY

The yummiest things I ate in Spain were:

The most disgusting things I ate in Spain were:

With my meals I like to drink:

Ask an adult for the receipt for one of your meals and stick it here:

HAPPY HOLIDAY

Travel journalists get to go all over the world to try out lots of places, hotels, food and things to do so they can help us decide where to go on holiday. While you're on the way home, why don't you pretend you're a reporter and write a review of your time in Spain? You'll need to say what was good and bad, what you most enjoyed and what you least enjoyed. It might be helpful to get some suggestions from everybody else travelling with you in case you've forgotten anything.

Happy Holidays!

Answers

Page 4

1. Malaga
2. Barcelona
3. Seville
4. Bilbao
5. Madrid
6. Ibiza

Page 11
(Spot the Difference)

1. The left-hand stall awning has changed colour.
2. There is a box where the melons were.
3. There is a boy shopping.
4. The pigeons have flown away.
5. There is a patch on the right-hand stall awning.
6. A peg on the right-hand awning is missing.
7. Sandi's pocket is missing.
8. The fish is upside down.
9. The banana on the box is missing.
10. The bones in the ham have gone.

Page 18 (Counting in Spanish)

Cinco	Cuatro	Seis
Tres	Uno	Dos

Page 23 (Word Search)

S	A	I	C	A	R	G	U
E	F	B	C	I	T	A	A
R	A	I	A	A	I	I	C
A	B	I	E	R	T	O	A
M	E	Z	R	S	C	C	T
A	S	U	A	H	T	O	C
L	A	T	O	C	E	A	A
A	I	S	E	L	G	I	L
C	H	U	R	R	O	A	S

Sandi Toksvig's
TRAVEL GUIDE TO SPAIN

A RED FOX BOOK 978 1 862 30430 7

First published in Great Britain by Red Fox, an imprint of Random House Children's Books
A Random House Group Company

This edition published 2009

1 3 5 7 9 10 8 6 4 2

Text copyright © Sandi Toksvig, 2009   Illustrations copyright © Dynamo, 2009   Design by Dynamo

The right of Sandi Toksvig to be identified as the author of this work has been
asserted in accordance with the Copyright, Designs and Patents Act 1988.

Red Fox Books are published by Random House Children's Books, 61–63 Uxbridge Road, London W5 5SA

www.kidsatrandomhouse.co.uk   www.rbooks.co.uk

Addresses for companies within The Random House Group Limited can be found at:
www.randomhouse.co.uk/offices.htm

THE RANDOM HOUSE GROUP Limited Reg. No. 954009

A CIP catalogue record for this book is available from the British Library.

Printed and bound in China

Photography: ©Shutterstock

Stephanie Strathdee, Graca Victoria, Peter Baxter, Carolina, Serge Lamere, Elias H Debbas II, Solodovinka Elena,
Photocreate, Absolut, Ljupco Smokovski, Jean Morrison, Elke Dennis, Parpalea Catalin, Nicole Weiss,
Peter Doomen, Jean Morrison, Marcel Gabriel Domenichelli, Dhoxax, Elena Aliaga, Carsten Reisinger